SECOND GRADE SCIENCE
SEMESTER B

ACCELERATE EDUCATION

Table of Contents

Module 19 1

Module 20 5

Module 21 9

Module 22 12

Module 23 16

Module 24 22

Module 25 25

Module 27 27

Module 28 28

Module 29 33

Module 30 35

Module 31 45

Module 32 47

Module 34 49

Module 35 51

Cutout Worksheets 53

This workbook contains all of the worksheets found in the Science 2 Semester B course. To see the worksheet in color, view it online within the lessons. For any worksheets containing cutting activities, they can be found in the "Cutout Worksheets" section.

© 2023 by Accelerate Education
Visit us on the Web at www.accelerate.education

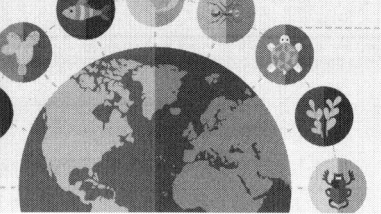

SCIENCE

Name: _____ Date: _____

Events That Quickly Change the Earth

Directions: Use what you know about events that quickly change the Earth to complete the activities below.

1. Name two changes to the land that happen quickly. Give examples of how the land can change quickly after each event.

a.

b.

2. With the help of your learning coach, pick either a volcanic eruption or an earthquake, and create a demonstration of it. Explain how you created the model, including the materials you used. Then explain how these quick changes can affect the Earth.

a. Materials used:	

b. What steps did you take to recreate this event?	

c. Explain how this event can change the Earth's surface.	

19.1 Quickly Changing Earth

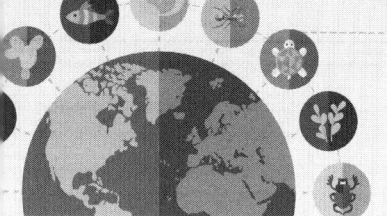

SCIENCE

Name: _____ Date: _____

Events That Slowly Change the Earth

Directions: Take a walk outside and look for evidence that a slow change has affected the land or an object around you. You may find smooth stones, a statue, a sidewalk, or another item that has changed from its original form. Then, answer the questions that follow.

1. Fill in the chart below using the objects you found. Be specific with what you observed and with what you think occurred.

Objects	Observation	What occurred?

Next Page

3

19.2 Slowly Changing Earth

2. Look at the images in the chart below. Describe what the land will look like after each slow change occurs.

Before	Event Occurring	What will it look like after the change?

19.2 Slowly Changing Earth

4

SCIENCE

Name: _____ Date: _____

Rock Classification

Directions: Observe the properties of the rocks in the table below. You can see the colors of the rocks in the lesson. Describe each property based on your observations. Then answer the question below the table.

	Color	Shape	Texture	Size
Rock A				
Rock B				
Rock C				
Rock D				

Which rocks would you classify into the same groups based on their properties?

_____

_____

_____

_____

5

20.1 Rocks

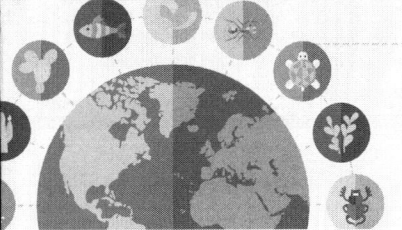

SCIENCE

Name: _____ Date: _____

Soil Observations

Directions: Look closely at the soil samples below. Record your observations about texture in the table below. For Sample 4, collect a soil sample from around your home. You will also need a cup and some water. Draw or upload a picture of the soil and record the texture in the table. Then answer the questions below.

	Picture	Texture
Sample 1		
Sample 2		
Sample 3		
Sample 4		

1. Do you think the soil you collected would hold water well? Why or why not?

_____
_____
_____

2. Put your soil in a cup and add some water to the cup. Write down your observations!

_____
_____

20.2 Soil

6

SCIENCE

Name: _____ Date: _____

Stop Erosion

Directions: Plan, design, and build your own solutions for erosion. Then, answer the questions about your solution.

Gather your materials:

- shallow tray, pan, or tub
- soil
- small cardboard box
- water
- your choice of barrier materials

1. Follow these directions to create your solution.
   a. Fill your tray, pan, or tub with soil, and make a slope or small hill.
   b. Put your cardboard box (house) on top of the soil at the bottom of the hill.
   c. Collect materials from around your home to build a solution to prevent the soil from washing away the house.
   d. Test your design by pouring water down your slope or hill as if it's raining.
   e. Use your mouth to blow air around your design as if it's windy.
   f. Record your results in the chart below.

Materials used	
Draw and label your design or upload a picture.	
Results	

Next Page

7

20.3 Preventing Erosion

2. Why do you think your design worked or did not work?

_____

3. What can you do differently next time to help improve your solution for erosion?

_____

SCIENCE

Name: _____ Date: _____

Earth vs. Space

Directions: Use the boxes below to draw a picture of what each activity would look like with gravity and without gravity.

Activity	With Gravity	Without Gravity
1. kicking a ball		
2. throwing a frisbee		
3. jumping on a trampoline		
4. going down a slide		
5. riding a bike		

21.3 Gravity

SCIENCE

Name: _____ Date: _____

Water Bottle Drop

Directions: Perform an experiment to investigate whether or not the mass of an object affects gravity by following the steps below.

1. What do you think will happen when you drop a full bottle of water and a half-filled bottle of water from the same height at the same time? Which one will land first?

   Write out your hypothesis:
   _____
   _____
   _____
   _____

2. Follow the steps:

   a. Use the table below to circle your predictions.
   b. Prepare two plastic water bottles. Make sure they are the exact same size and shape. Fill one bottle completely with water and the other bottle halfway.
   c. Holding your arms out, with one bottle in each hand, drop the bottles from the same height at the same time.
   d. Record your observations in the table below.
   e. Repeat the experiment three times.

	Predict: Circle which bottle will land first.	Test: Write down what happened.
Drop #1	FULL HALF	
Drop #2	FULL HALF	
Drop #3	FULL HALF	

Next Page

21.4 Project: Water Bottle Drop

3. Did the amount of water in each bottle affect which landed first? Circle your answer.

YES   NO

4. What conclusion can you draw about mass and gravity?

_____
_____
_____
_____
_____

5. Try removing or adding water to one of the bottles. Drop the bottles again. Did you get the same result or a different result? Why?

_____
_____
_____
_____
_____
_____
_____
_____
_____
_____
_____
_____

SCIENCE

Name: _____ Date: _____

Observing Insects

Directions: Look at the following pictures. Then complete each chart.

1.

What kind of insect is this picture showing?	How can you tell?	What do you think the insects are doing?

2.

What kind of insect is this picture showing?	How can you tell?	What do you think the insects are doing?

Next Page

22.1 Characteristics of Insects

12

3.

What kind of insect is this picture showing?	How can you tell?	What do you think the insects are doing?

22.1 Characteristics of Insects

SCIENCE

Name: _____ Date: _____

Observing Ants

Directions: Look at the picture below. The sections of the ant colony are numbered.

1. Think about what the ants are doing in each section.

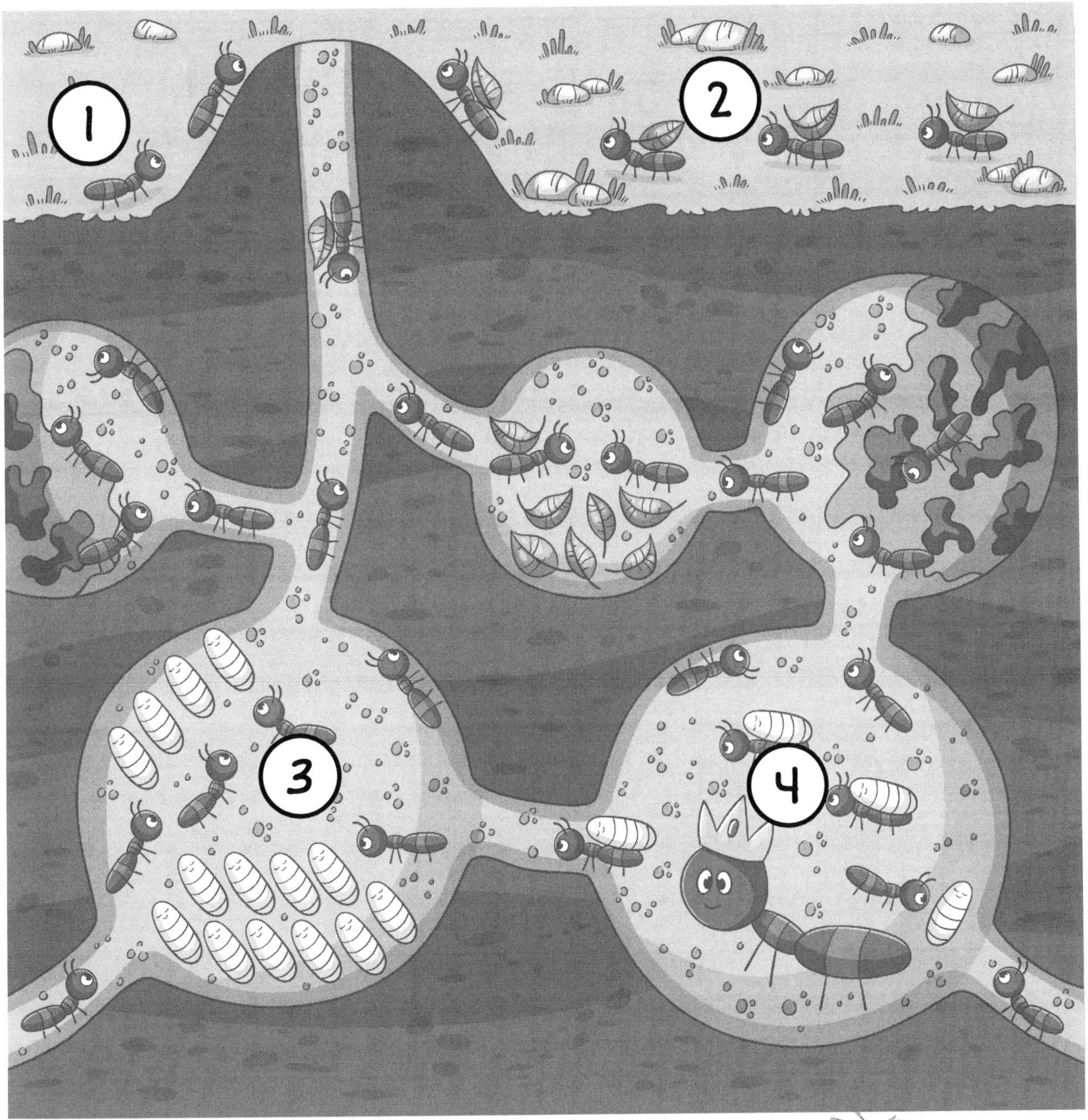

Next Page

22.2 Ant Behavior

14

2. Complete the sentences by filling in the blanks.

   a. In section 1, the soldiers are _____.

   b. In section 2, the _____ are bringing food to the nest.

   c. In section 3, the workers are _____

   and _____.

   d. In section 4, the _____ is laying eggs.

3. Pick one type of ant behavior from the lesson that you thought was interesting. Draw a picture of it.

4. What type of behavior is your ant doing?

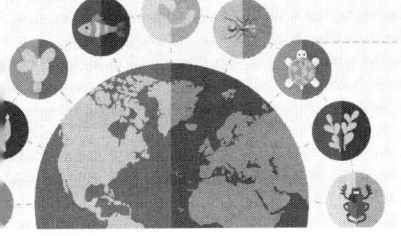

SCIENCE

Name: _____ Date: _____

Hive for a Home

Directions: Design a honeycomb. Draw at least ten six-sided cells below, just like the honeycomb in a beehive! In five of those cells, write a fact about bees that you learned from today's lesson.

23.1 Bee Behavior

16

SCIENCE

Name: _____ Date: _____

Spreading Seeds

Directions: What are some different ways that pollen and seeds can be spread from plant to plant? Draw four different ways you learned about. Write 1-2 sentences under each picture to explain the pollination process.

Next Page

17

23.2 Pollination and Seeds

23.2 Pollination and Seeds

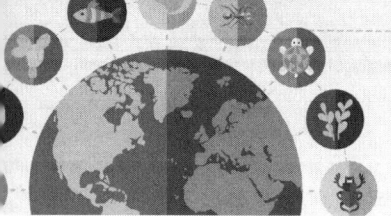

SCIENCE

Name: _____ Date: _____

Design a Pollinator

Directions: Create a handmade bee pollinator by following the steps of the engineering design process. Your bee pollinator should help solve the problem of spreading seeds or pollen as animals or insects do.

Step 1: Ask

1. What is the problem you are trying to solve?

   _____
   _____
   _____
   _____

Step 2: Imagine

2. What do you think your handmade bee pollinator should look like?

   _____
   _____
   _____
   _____

3. What materials can you use to help solve the problem?

   _____
   _____
   _____
   _____

Next Page

23.3 Engineering Pollination

Step 3: Plan

4. Sketch your design in the space below.

Step 4: Create

5. Build your model using the steps and materials in your plan. Take a picture of your creation and paste it below.

23.3 Engineering Pollination

Step 5: Test

6. Test your design! Use your model to collect pollen from one plant and move it to another to see how effective it is. Take notes below on what worked and did not work well.

_____
_____
_____
_____
_____
_____
_____

Step 6: Improve

7. After testing your design, what changes will you make?

_____
_____
_____
_____
_____
_____
_____

8. Retest your design. Was the new design more or less successful than the first?

_____
_____
_____
_____
_____
_____
_____

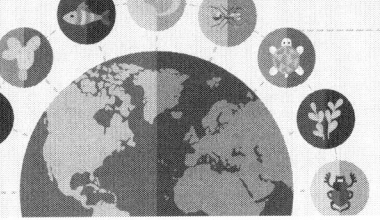

SCIENCE

Name: _____ Date: _____

Animal Teamwork

Directions: In this lesson, you learned about animal cooperation. Complete the activity below using what you know!

1. Read the different scenarios below. Color the boxes that represent animal cooperation.

A lion is looking for something to eat. It spots a zebra eating grass. The lion slowly creeps into in the brush, so the zebra does not see him. The lion waits until it is time to attack.	A honey guide is a bird that loves honey but has a tough time getting into beehives. These birds lead honey badgers to the beehive. So, the honey badgers can get the beehive for themselves and their bird friend.
Bears like to eat fish out of the rivers during the salmon run, which is when salmon swim back upriver to lay their eggs. The bears will wait and fish for the salmon during this time of year.	A bird named an oxpecker hangs around a zebra to eat the ticks and other insects that like to land on the zebra's body. This bird also alerts the zebra if it is in danger.

2. How do animals cooperate to help increase their chances of survival?

   _____
   _____
   _____
   _____

24.1 Animal Cooperation

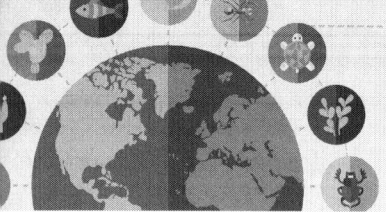
SCIENCE

Name: _____ Date: _____

Animal Helpers

Directions: In the boxes below, draw one example of animals helping humans and one example of humans helping animals. Below each picture, write a few sentences to explain how they are helping each other.

Animals Helping Humans	Humans Helping Animals

23

24.2 Relationships Between Humans and Animals

SCIENCE

Name: _____ Date: _____

Cooperating Animals

Directions: In this lesson, you have learned about dolphins and prairie dogs and how they cooperate to ensure their survival. Answer the questions below about either dolphins or prairie dogs.

1. Draw a picture of the animal cooperating with others in its group.

2. Write one or two sentences to explain how the animals are cooperating.

_____
_____
_____
_____
_____

24.3 Dolphins and Prairie Dogs

24

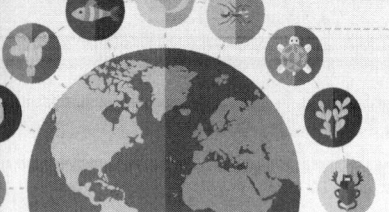
SCIENCE

Name: _____ Date: _____

Identifying Carnivores

Directions: Use what you learned about carnivores to complete the activities below.

1. Look at the images below. Circle the animals that you think eat meat.

eagle

cow

shark

panther

deer

grasshopper
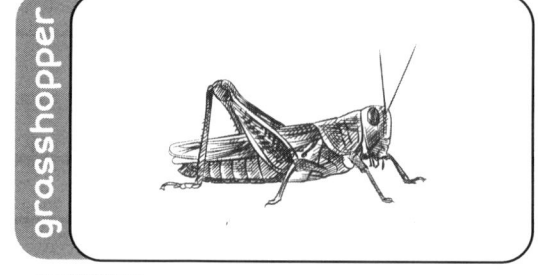

dog

penguin

Next Page

25　　25.2 Carnivores

2. Pick two of the animals and explain why you think they eat meat.

_____
_____
_____
_____
_____
_____
_____
_____
_____
_____
_____
_____
_____
_____
_____
_____
_____
_____
_____
_____

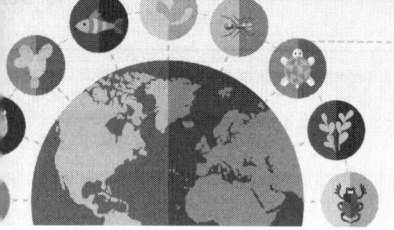

SCIENCE

Name: _____ Date: _____

Insect vs. Amphibian Life Cycles

Directions: Create a Venn diagram. Write down the similarities and differences between the life cycle stages of salamanders and ladybugs. Put "Salamanders" on the left side and "Ladybugs" on the right. Then, you will label the overlapping part "Both". Include at least three things in each part of the Venn diagram.

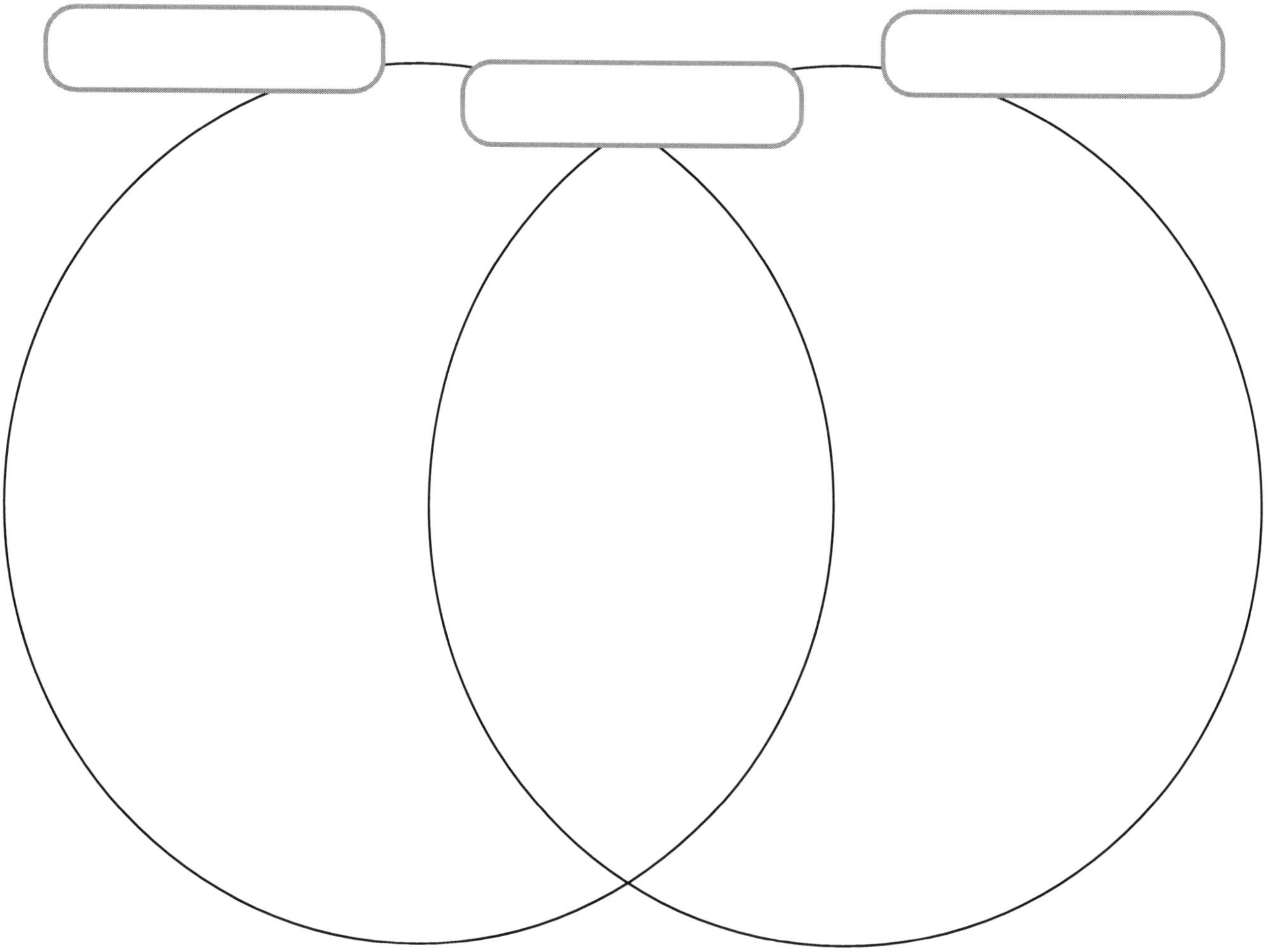

SCIENCE

Name: _____ Date: _____

Parts of a Tree

Directions: Using what you know about trees and leaves, complete the activities below.

1. Use the words in the word bank to label the parts of the tree below. Then, collect two leaves from two different trees and describe them.

> leaves   roots
> branch   trunk   crown

PARTS OF A TREE

Next Page

28.1 Trees and Leaves

28

2. Collect a couple leaves from two different types of local trees and paste them in the boxes labeled Leaf. Write a description about the leaves in the boxes as well. Next, draw and describe the trees which the leaves came from in the boxes labeled Tree.

Leaf	Tree

Leaf	Tree

28.1 Trees and Leaves

SCIENCE

Name: _____ Date: _____

Tree Patterns

Directions: Draw and color the different types of trees below. Then answer the questions about deciduous and coniferous trees.

1. Color the deciduous trees to match the seasons shown in the table.

Summer	Fall	Winter	Spring

2. Draw a coniferous tree.

Next Page

28.2 Plant Patterns   **30**

3. Give one example of how a deciduous tree and a coniferous tree are similar.

4. Give one example of how a deciduous tree and a coniferous tree are different.

SCIENCE

Name: _____   Date: _____

Bean Life Cycle

Directions: Use words from the word bank to label the parts of the bean cycle. Then draw arrows to show the direction of the cycle.

| seed | flower | germination |
| seedling | adult plant | seed pod |

1. _____

2. _____

3. _____

4. _____

5. _____

6. _____

28.3 Life Cycle of a Bean

SCIENCE

Name: _____ Date: _____

Create a Plant

Directions: It is time to design your own plant! Use the boxes below to draw pictures showing what your plant will look like during each stage of its growth. Label each stage using these words: seed, sprout, seedling, plant.

Stage 1: _____

Stage 2: _____

My Plant's Name: _____

Stage 3: _____

Stage 4: _____

33

29.1 Seeds All Around

SCIENCE

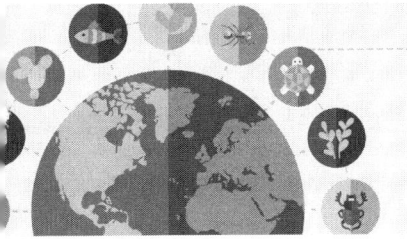

Name: _____   Date: _____

Predict Plant Growth

Directions: A science class wants to test and observe what will happen if plants do not have their basic needs met. The students record what they did or did not give their plants.

1. Use the chart below to make predictions about what will happen to each plant.

	Nutrients: What was the seed planted in?	Water: yes or no	Sunlight: yes or no	Predict: Will this plant grow?	Sketch what this plant will look like.
Kim	rocks	yes	no		
Carl	soil	yes	yes		
Sam	soil	yes	no		

2. Which student's plant will grow the most? Why?

_____
_____
_____
_____
_____

29.2 How Plants Grow

SCIENCE

Name: _____ Date: _____

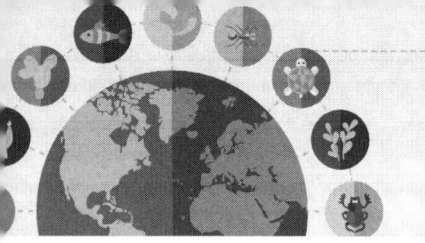

Test the Soil

Directions: You will create a step-by-step plan on determining if different soil types can affect plant growth with the materials below.

Materials:
- three paper cups
- seeds (1 packet of beets, tomatoes, lettuce, or squash)
- water
- three different soil types from around your home (ex: silt, loam, clay, potting soil)
- ruler

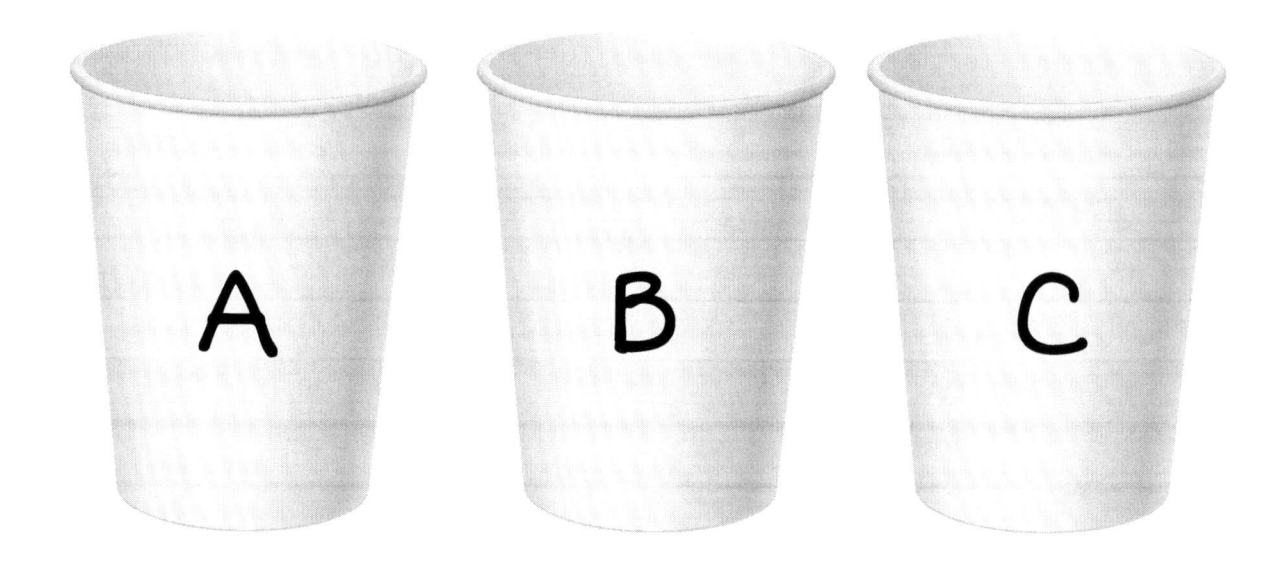

Remember: In an experiment, you need to make sure you are testing only one thing. You need to keep everything else the same. This time, think about testing the soil type. The amount of water, light, size of the cup, and everything else must stay the same for each cup! Answer the following questions.

Next Page

1. What kinds of soil will you use?

   _____   _____   _____

2. What type of seed will you use?

   _____
   _____
   _____
   _____

3. How much water will you give each cup each day?

   _____
   _____
   _____
   _____

4. Where will you put your plants?

   _____
   _____
   _____
   _____

5. What will you measure to show health and growth?

   _____
   _____
   _____
   _____

Next Page

30.1 Soil Experiment

SCIENCE

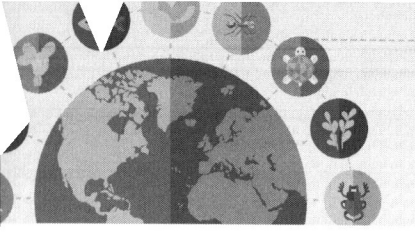

Name: _____   Date: _____

Watch Your Water

Directions: In this activity, you will create a plan to determine if the amount of water a plant gets affects plant growth with the materials below.

Materials:
- three paper cups marked A, B, and C
- marker
- seeds (1 packet of beets, tomatoes, lettuce, or squash)
- measuring cup or spoons
- soil
- ruler
- water

Remember: In an experiment, you need to make sure that you test only one thing. You must keep everything else the same. For this experiment, focus on how much water you give your plants. Keep the type and amount of soil, cup size, and sunlight the same for each plant.

Next Page

37

30.2 Water Experiment

1. How much water will you give to each plant?

   _____   _____   _____

2. Which type of soil will you use?

3. Where will you keep your plants so they receive sunlight?

4. How will you measure the amount of water each plant gets daily?

5. What will you measure to show health and growth?

30.2 Water Experiment

SCIENCE

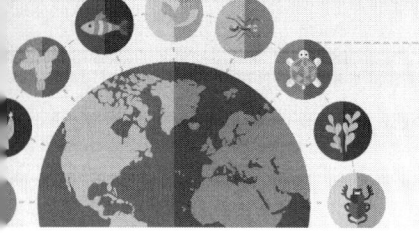

Name: _____ Date: _____

Sunlight for Plants

Directions: In this activity, you will create a plan to determine if the amount of sunlight a plant gets affects plant growth with the materials below.

Materials:
- three paper cups
- seeds (1 packet of beets, tomatoes, lettuce, or squash)
- water
- soil
- ruler

Remember: In an experiment, you need to make sure that you test only one thing. Everything else stays the same. For this experiment, focus on how much sunlight the plants get. Keep the type and amount of soil, cup size, and amount of water the same for each plant.

Next Page

39   30.3 Sun Experiment

1. Where will you place your plants during the experiment?

   _____   _____   _____

2. Which type of soil will you use?

3. How much water will you give each cup each day?

4. What will you measure to show health and growth?

5. How will you record the results of your plant growth?

6. What important question will you have answered for this experiment?

30.3 Sun Experiment

SCIENCE

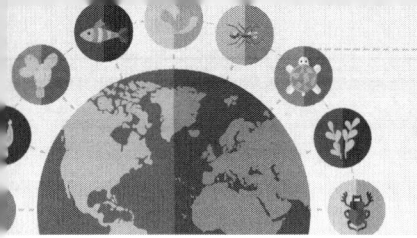

Name: _____ Date: _____

Planned Plant Experiment

Directions: Follow the steps in the lesson for the experiment you choose. Once your seeds have sprouted, measure your plants' heights with a ruler. Write your results and observations in the table below. Once your soil experiment is complete, answer the questions. Select only ONE section (Soil Experiment, Water Experiment, or Sunlight Experiment section) to complete.

Soil Experiment

Soil Table

Date	Soil A	Soil B	Soil C
Example: 2/15	green, small leaves, ½ inch	no leaves ½ inch	has not sprouted

Next Page

41 30.4 Project: Planned Plant Experiment

Questions

1. Which type of soil did your plants grow best in?
   _____
   _____

2. Why do you think that soil worked best?
   _____
   _____

3. Which type of soil did not work for your plants?
   _____
   _____

4. Why do you think that soil did not work well?
   _____
   _____

Water Experiment

Water Table

Date	Cup A Amount of Water	Cup B Amount of Water	Cup C Amount of Water
Example: 2/15	green, small leaves, ½ inch	no leaves ½ inch	has not sprouted

Next Page

30.4 Project: Planned Plant Experiment

Questions

1. Which cup had the best results?
   _____
   _____

2. Why do you think that cup had the best results?
   _____
   _____

3. How can you help the plants in the other cups thrive and grow stronger?
   _____
   _____
   _____

Sunlight Experiment

Sunlight Table

Date	Cup A Amount of Sunlight ____	Cup B Amount of Sunlight ____	Cup C Amount of Sunlight ____
Example: 2/15	green, small leaves, ½ inch	no leaves ½ inch	has not sprouted

Next Page

43 30.4 Project: Planned Plant Experiment

Questions

1. Which location did your plants grow best in?
   _____
   _____

2. Why do you think that spot worked best?
   _____
   _____

3. Which location did not help your plants grow?
   _____
   _____

4. Why do you think that spot did not work well?
   _____
   _____

30.4 Project: Planned Plant Experiment

SCIENCE

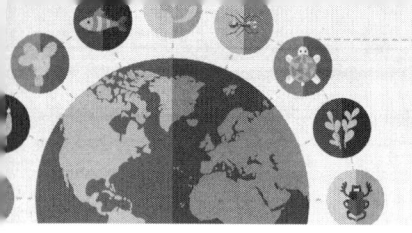

Name: _____ Date: _____

Investigating Heat and Light

Directions: Draw and describe what you predict will happen when either heat or light energy is added or taken away.

1. Before:	After heat energy is removed:
	_____

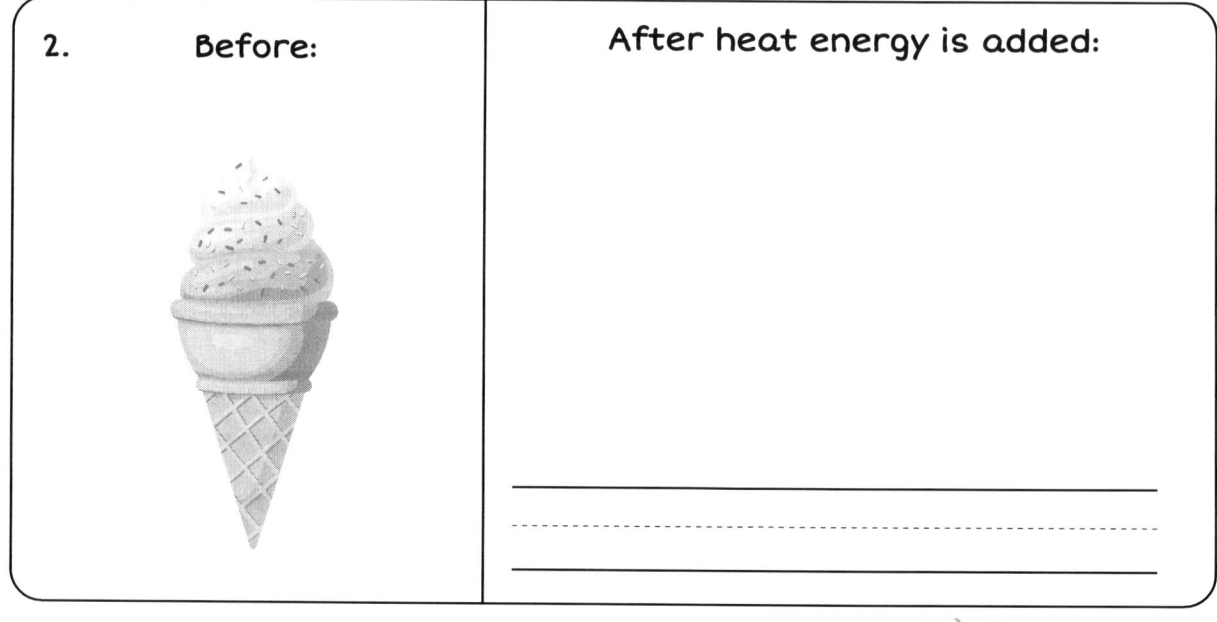

2. Before:	After heat energy is added:
	_____

Next Page

31.1 Light and Heat

3. Before:

After light energy is added:

4. Before:

After light energy is removed:

31.1 Light and Heat

SCIENCE

Name: _____   Date: _____

Renewable Resource Uses

Directions: Complete the table below by writing the uses for each renewable resource.

Renewable Resource	Picture	Uses
Sun		
trees		

Next Page

47　　　　　　　　　　　　　　　　　　　　32.3 Renewable Resources

Renewable Resource	Picture	Uses
water		
wind		

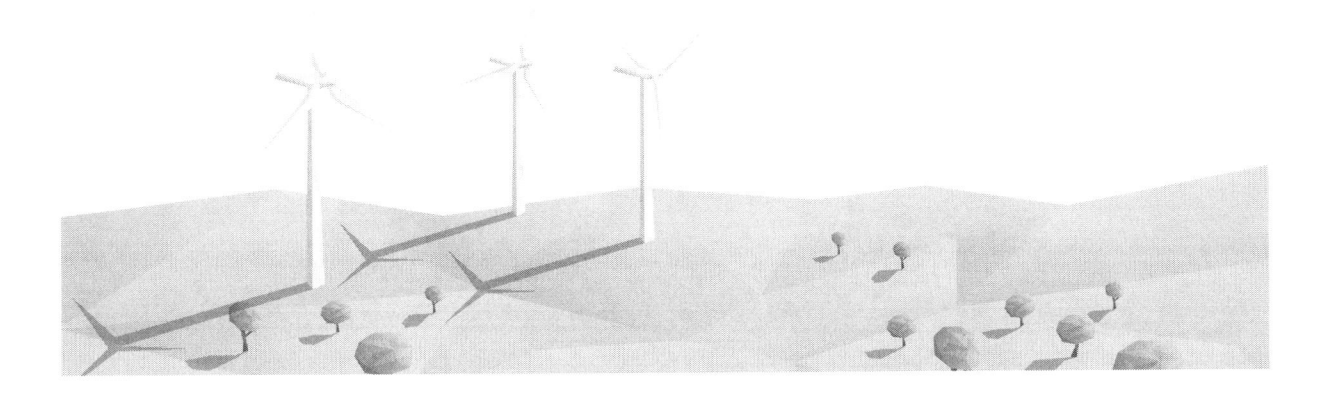

32.3 Renewable Resources

SCIENCE

Name: _____ Date: _____

Repurposing Materials

Directions: Look at the following items that are commonly thrown away. Write down two ways that the item could be repurposed.

Item	First Way	Second Way
glass jar		
milk jug		
egg carton		

Optional: If you have one of these items in your home, try to repurpose it using one of the ways you suggested!

49   34.2 The Four Rs

SCIENCE

Name: _____ Date: _____

Children Take Action!

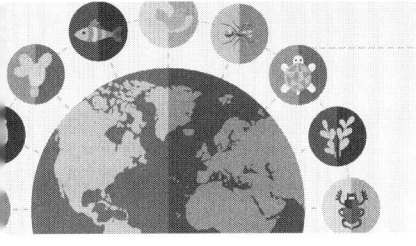

Directions: Design a poster that tells others about the importance of conserving water or electricity. Be sure to include a title and illustrations, and list or show ways that people can conserve.

34.3 Taking Action

SCIENCE

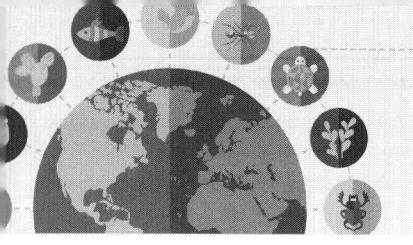

Name: _____ Date: _____

Design a Pollinator Garden

Directions: Use this page to help you plan and design your very own pollinator garden!

1. What kinds of plants will you plant in your garden and why?
   _____
   _____
   _____
   _____

2. Will you plant seeds or plants that are already grown?
   _____
   _____
   _____
   _____

3. How often will you water your garden?
   _____
   _____
   _____
   _____

4. Which types of animals do you hope to see spreading pollen in your garden?
   _____
   _____
   _____
   _____

Next Page

5. What will you do to make sure your garden stays healthy?

6. Draw a picture of your pollinator garden.

Optional: Plant your pollinator garden! If you have space and the materials, go ahead and plant your pollinator garden where you live.

35.1 Plant a Pollinator Garden

Cutout Worksheets

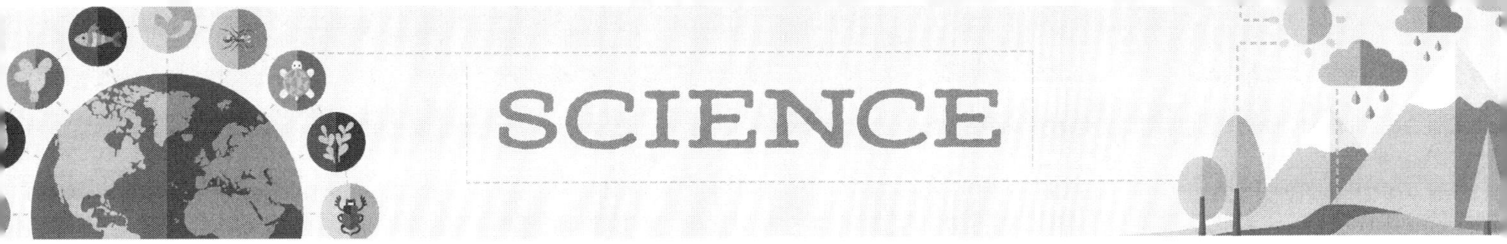

SCIENCE

Name: _____ Date: _____

Weathering and Soil

Directions: Use what you know about weathering and soil to complete the activities below.

1. Cut out the pictures at the bottom of the page that describe how weathering contributes to soil formation. Paste them in correct order in the chart.

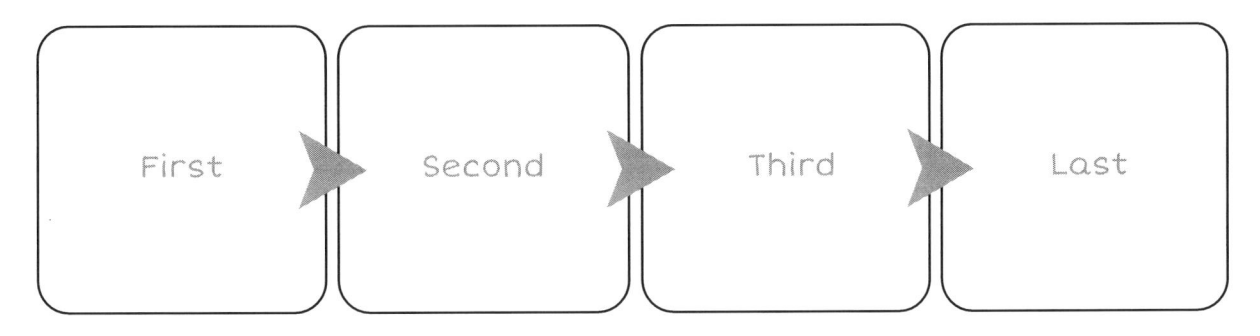

| First | ▶ | Second | ▶ | Third | ▶ | Last |

2. Describe how you would create a model of water eroding land.

_____
_____
_____
_____
_____

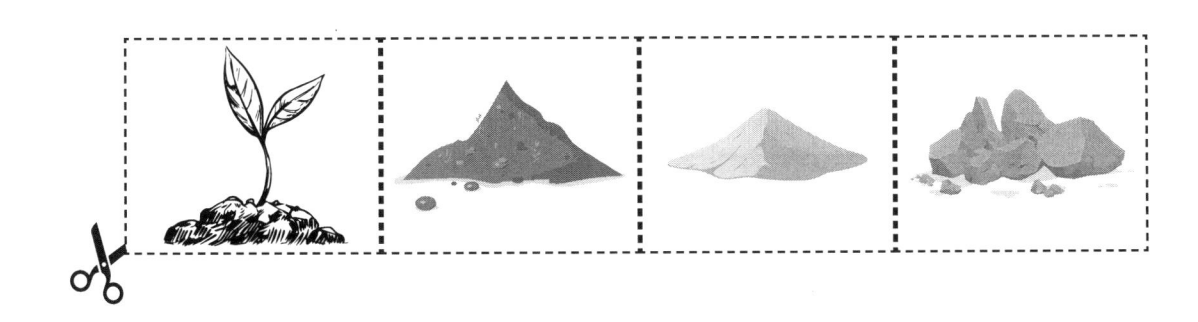

19.3 Weathering & Erosion

SCIENCE

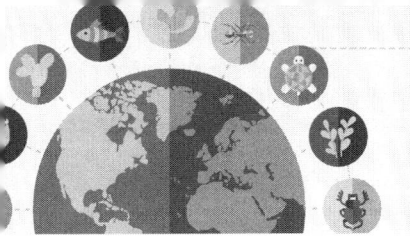

Name: _____ Date: _____

Slide, Roll, Spin Assignment

Directions: Practice comparing the types of motion that different objects make. Cut out the pictures below along the dotted lines. Paste each picture into one of the three categories. Does it show sliding, rolling, or spinning? Use the blank square to draw your own example of sliding, rolling, or spinning. Paste it in the correct column.

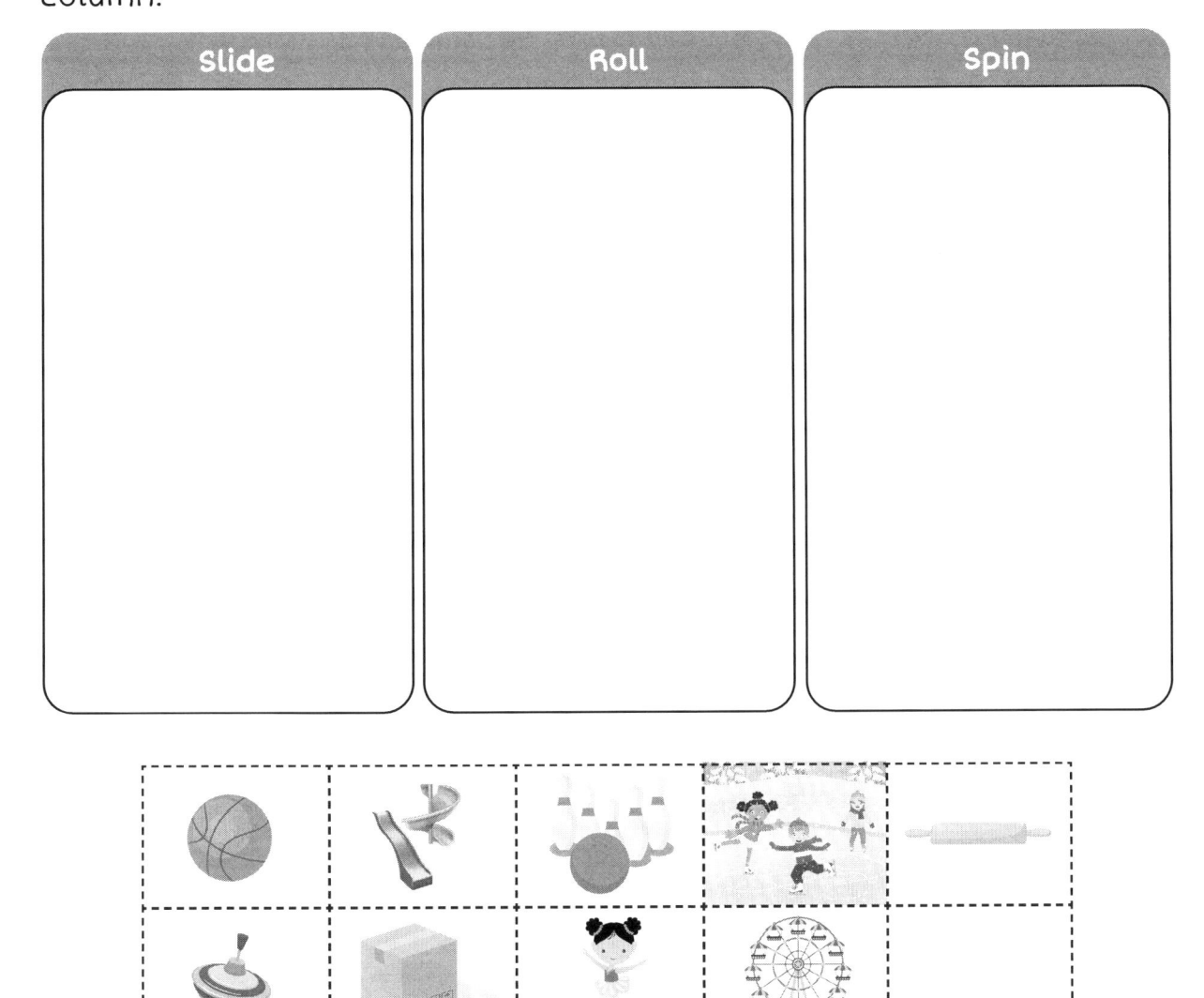

Slide	Roll	Spin

21.1 Objects Moving

56

SCIENCE

Name: _____   Date: _____

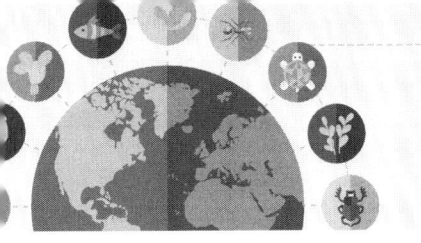

Spider Webs

Directions: Using what you learned about spiders in the lesson, complete the following activities.

1. Look at the spider web below. Trace the web with your pencil. Then cut out the images below and place them on your spider web to show how spiders catch their food.

2. Describe how you could create a model of a spider web. Include the materials you would use and explain why you would use them.

_____
_____
_____
_____
_____
_____

22.3 Spider Webs

2. Go outside and find a food chain to observe. You can also think about a food chain from the lesson. Draw the food chain in the box below. Use arrows to show how the energy flows from start to finish. Then describe how the energy flows through the food chain.

25.1 Animal Food Chains

SCIENCE

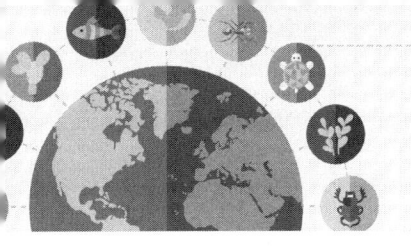

Name: _____   Date: _____

Birds of Prey Food Chain

Directions: Cut out the images below along the dotted lines. Paste them in the correct order in the food chain chart below. Draw arrows between the boxes to show the flow of energy.

Food Chain for Birds of Prey

| eagle | grass | snake | mouse | sun |

25.3 Birds of Prey

SCIENCE

Name: _____   Date: _____

Meat or Plants

Directions: Cut out the pictures and phrases below along the dotted lines. Decide whether they are or describe carnivores, herbivores, or both. Sort them into the correct categories in the Venn diagram.

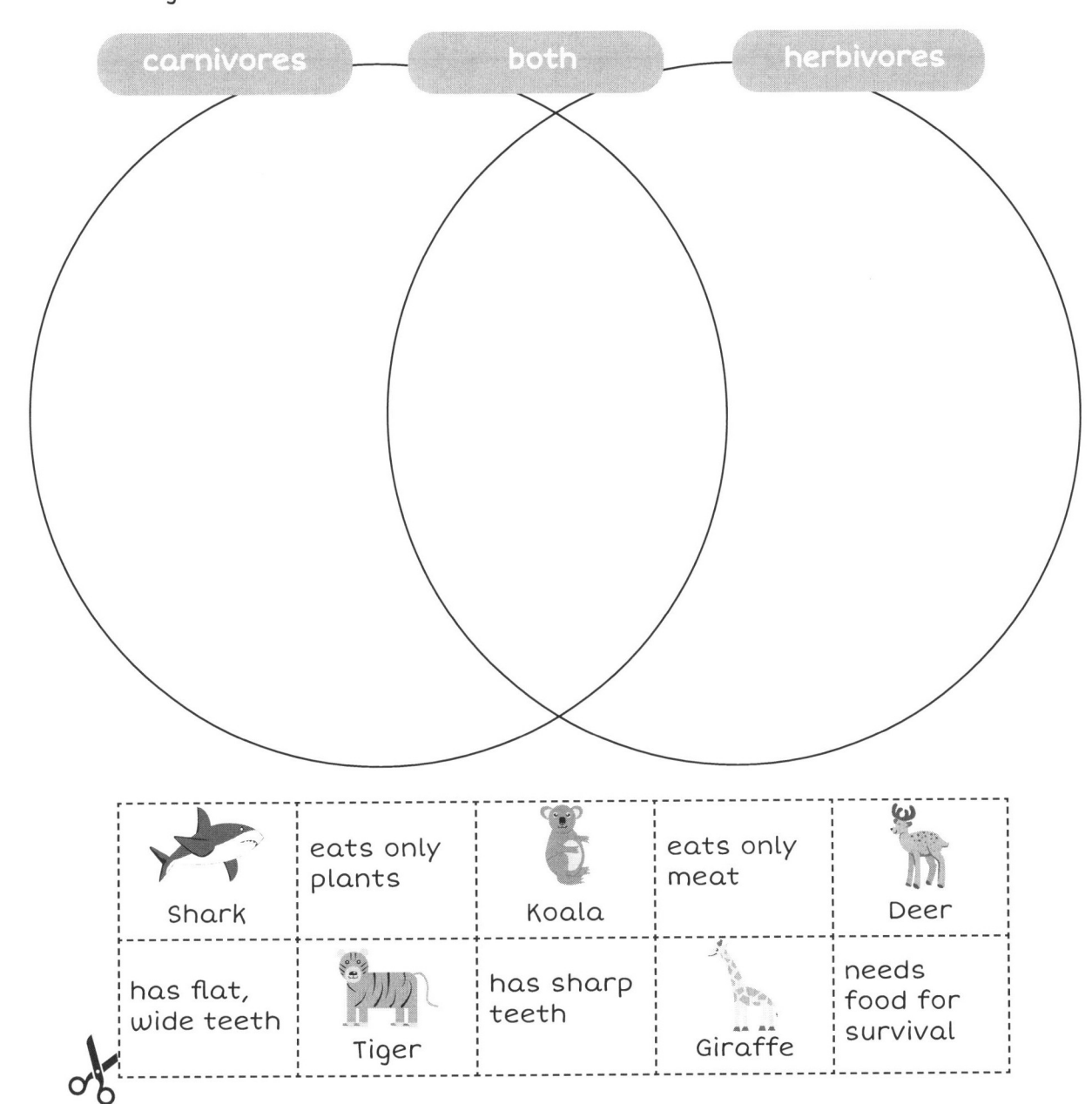

carnivores — **both** — **herbivores**

Shark	eats only plants	Koala	eats only meat	Deer
has flat, wide teeth	Tiger	has sharp teeth	Giraffe	needs food for survival

26.1 Herbivores

68

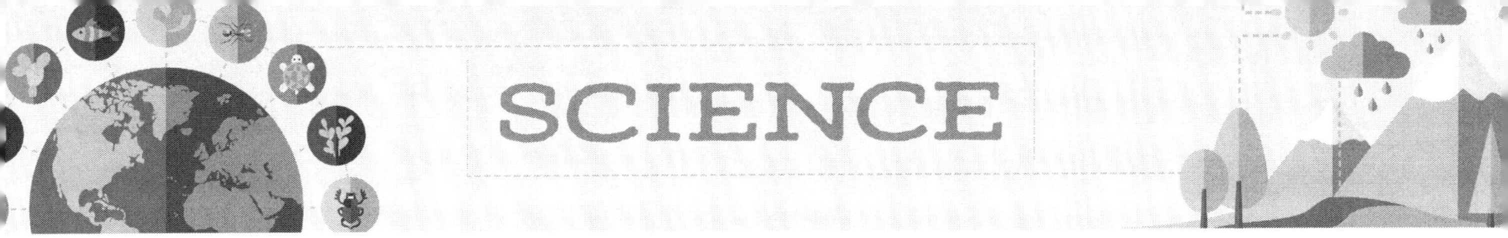

SCIENCE

Name: _____ Date: _____

Animal Sort

Directions: Decide whether each animal is an herbivore, a carnivore, or an omnivore. Then create a food chain.

1. Cut out the pictures of animals below along the dotted lines. Sort the animals into the correct categories in the table.

Herbivores	Carnivores	Omnivores

2. Draw and label a food chain below using one of the animals from your sort.

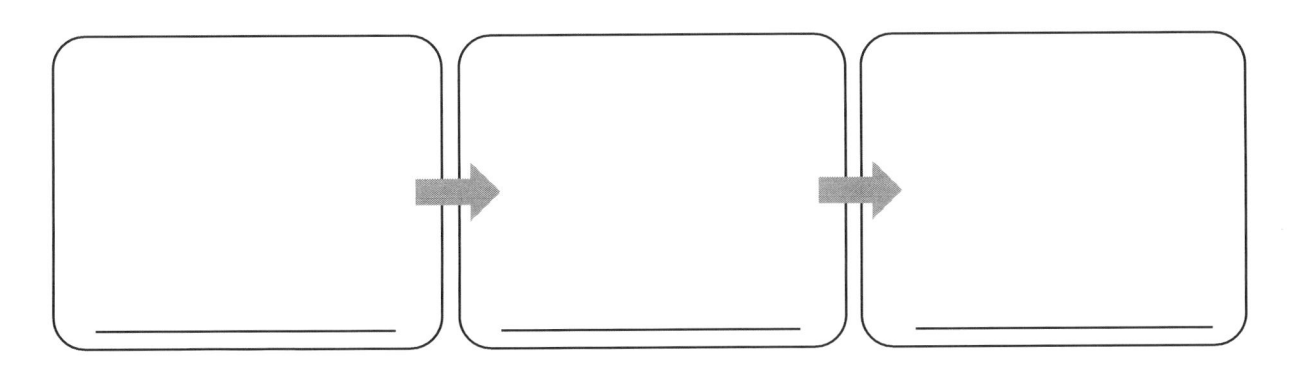

Anteater | Skunk | Monkey | Tiger | Deer | Shark
Koala | Lion | Kiwi | Elephant | Bear | Giraffe

26.2 Omnivores

SCIENCE

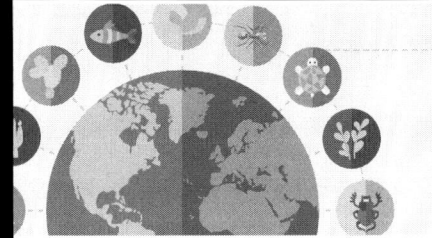

Name: _____   Date: _____

My Food Chain

Directions: Today, you will create your own paper food chain! Choose your favorite food that comes from animals. Create a food chain to show how the energy is transferred between the links like this example.

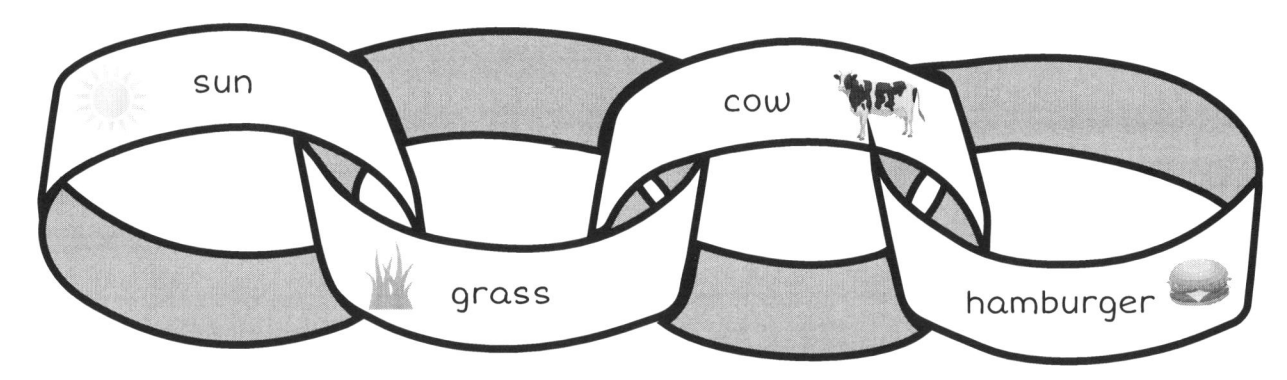

sun — grass — cow — hamburger

Draw and label the pictures of your chosen food and the food chain on the strips of paper provided below. Attach the strips together in the correct order. Take a picture of your food chain and turn it in to your teacher when you are finished.

26.3 Food for Humans

SCIENCE

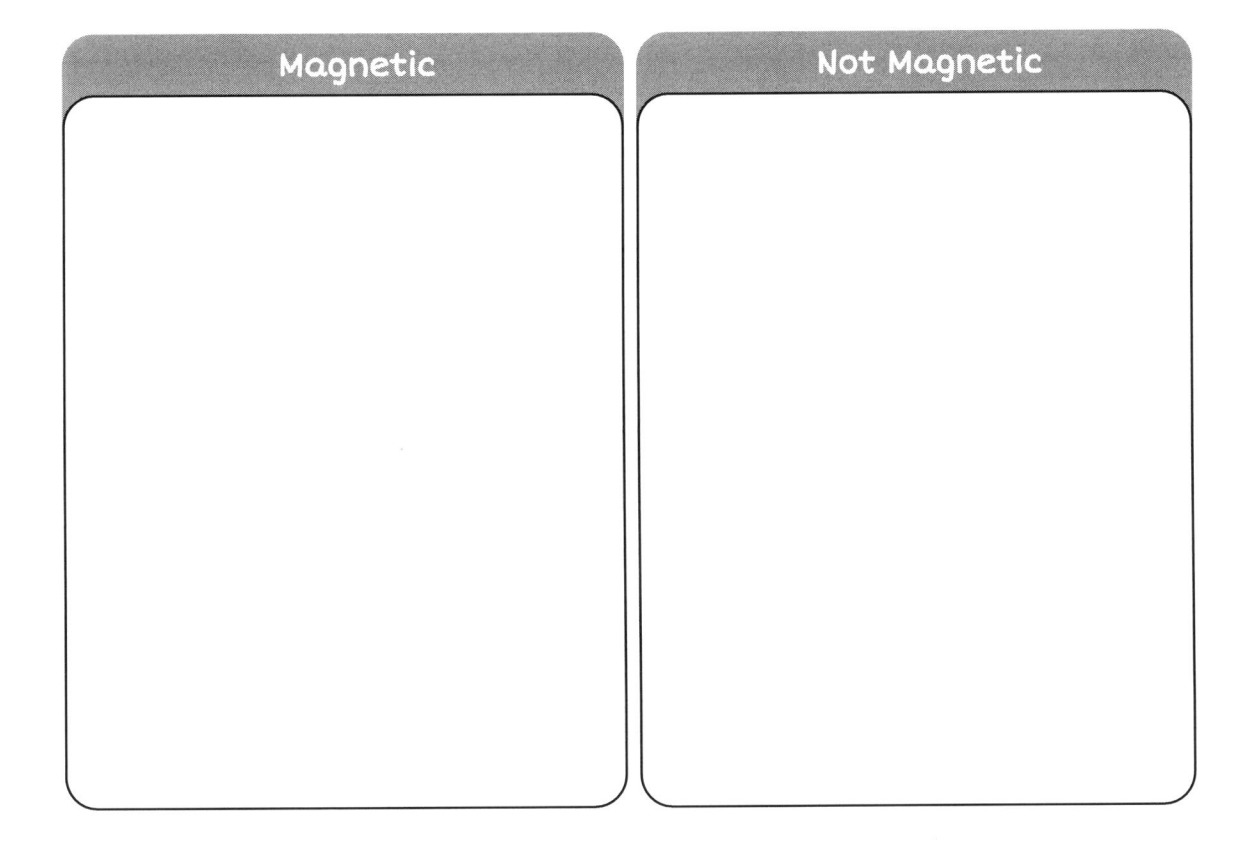

Name: _____ Date: _____

Classify Objects by Their Magnetism

Directions: Practice sorting objects based on their magnetism. Cut out the pictures below along the dotted lines. Paste each picture into one of the two categories. Which items are magnetic?

Magnetic	Not Magnetic

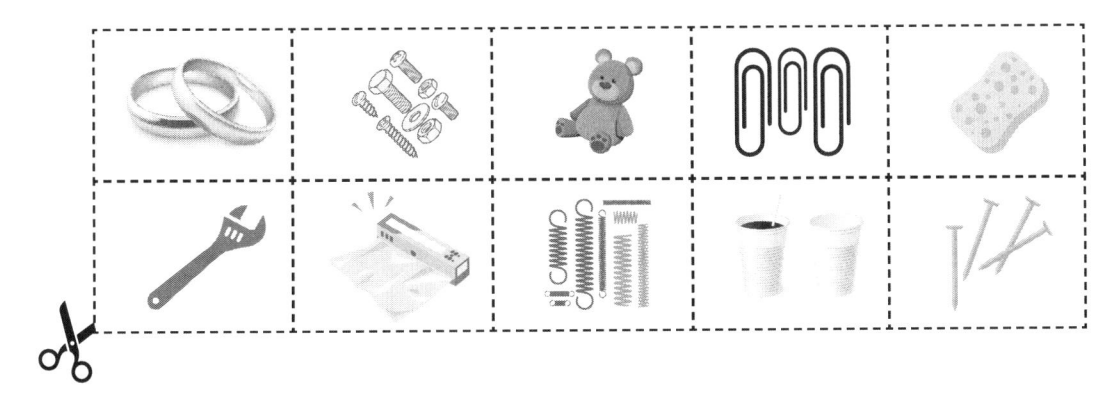

21.2 Magnets

58

SCIENCE

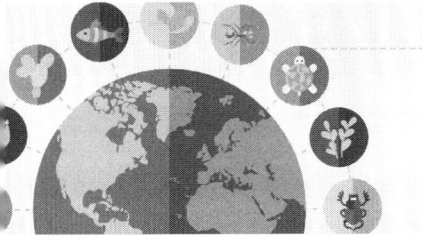

Name: _____   Date: _____

Life Cycle of a Frog

Directions: Cut out both the picture cards and the text cards at the bottom of the page along the dotted lines. Paste them in the correct order to show the life cycle of a frog. Label each stage of the life cycle with the correct word: egg, tadpole, young frog, adult frog.

Stage 1:	Stage 2:	Stage 3:	Stage 4:

| Tadpoles hatch from the eggs. They have gills to help them breathe underwater. | The tadpole grows front legs, and its tail gets shorter. It also grows lungs to breathe air. | The young frog grows into an adult and will help repeat the life cycle again. | A frog lays her eggs in the water. They will hatch in about one to three weeks. |

27.1 Tadpoles to Frogs

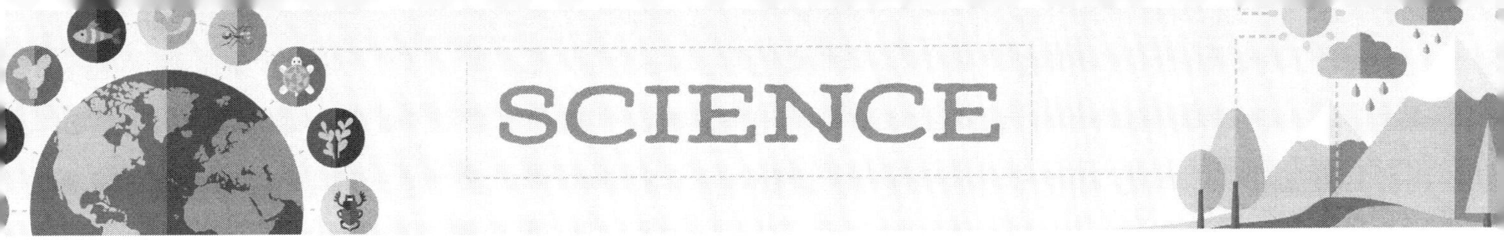

SCIENCE

Name: _____ Date: _____

Life Cycle of a Grasshopper

Directions: Cut out the life cycle pictures below along the dotted lines. Paste them in the boxes in the correct order. On the line provided, label each stage using one of these words: eggs, nymph, adult. Below each box, write a description of each stage of the life cycle.

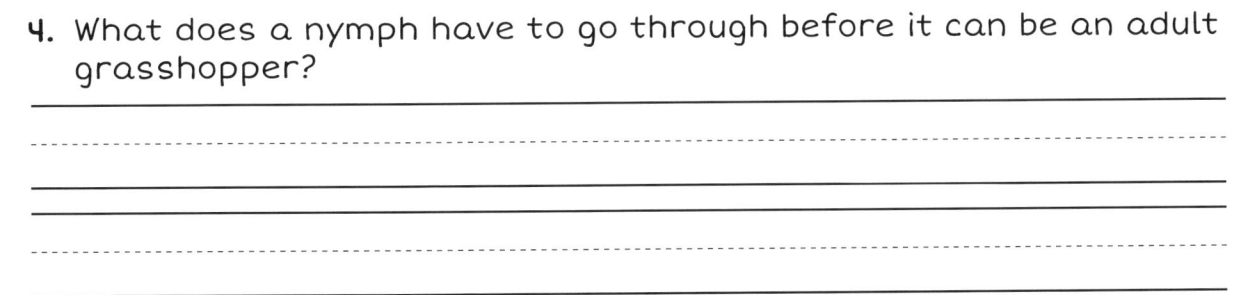

1. Stage 1:	2. Stage 2:	3. Stage 3:
_____	_____	_____

4. What does a nymph have to go through before it can be an adult grasshopper?

_____
_____
_____

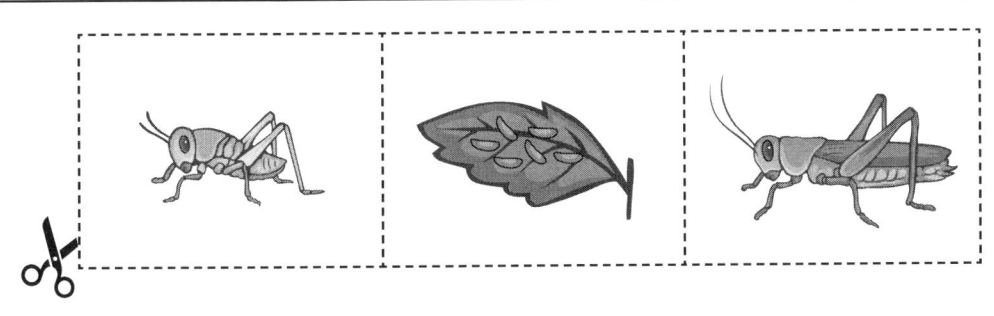

27.2 Grasshopper Life Cycle

76

SCIENCE

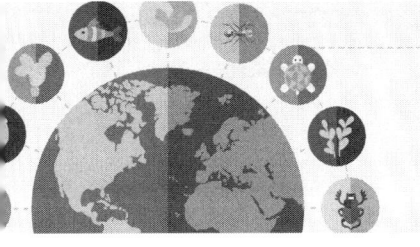

Name: _____ Date: _____

Life Cycle of a Butterfly

Directions: Cut out the life cycle pictures below along the dotted lines. Paste them in the correct order in the boxes below. Label each stage using one of these words: eggs, larva, pupa, butterfly. Then write a description of each stage in the box under the picture.

Stage 1:	Stage 2:	Stage 3:	Stage 4:

27.3 Caterpillar to Butterfly

78

SCIENCE

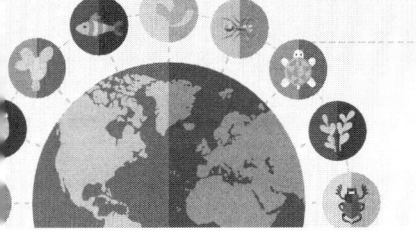

Name: _____ Date: _____

Different Plants, Different Needs

Directions: Read the clues to learn about each plant and one of its individual needs. Cut out the pictures on the next page along the dotted lines. Paste the correct picture in each box, and label it with the correct title: tree, shrub, creeper, climber, or herb.

Type: _____

Great Oak

This plant grows tall and has a hard, wooden stem.

Individual need: The Great Oak must have at least four hours of sunlight every day.

Type: _____

Ivy

This plant grows tall along fences and walls.

Individual need: Ivy needs more water in the spring and summer.

Type: _____

Rosebush

This plant grows short, hard stems and branches that stay low to the ground.

Individual need: A young rosebush needs water every two to three days.

Next Page

29.3 Types of Plants

Type: _____

Basil

This plant has a small, soft stem. It is often used to flavor food or to make medicine.

Individual need: Basil must spend all day in the Sun.

Type: _____

Strawberries

This plant grows along the ground. It has a stem that can bend.

Individual need: Strawberry plants have shallow roots, so they need water every day.

29.3 Types of Plants

SCIENCE

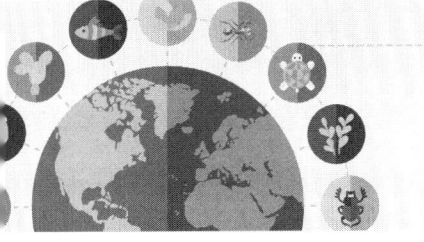

Name: _____ Date: _____

Energy Changing

Directions: Cut out the pictures on the next page along the dotted lines. Paste them in the correct places to form picture equations to show how energy can cause change.

Here's an example of how heat is added to bread to make toast.

Adding heat:

1. **Adding light:**

2. **Adding heat:**

3. **Removing heat:**

Next Page

31.2 Changes in Energy

84

4. Removing light:

5. Adding heat:

31.2 Changes in Energy

SCIENCE

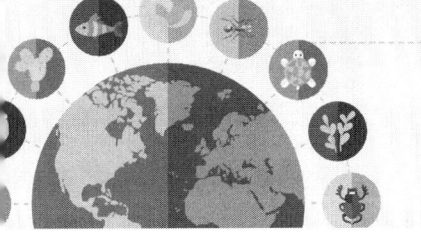

Name: _____   Date: _____

Using Energy

Directions: Apply what you know about using energy to complete the activities below.

1. Cut out the pictures on the next page along the dotted lines. Paste the pictures in the correct row. You should have two pictures in each row. Then, fill in the missing information in the chart.

Form of Energy	Definition	Examples
Heat		
Light		
Sound		
Electrical		

Next Page

31.3 Uses of Energy

88

2. Think about the ways in which you use energy every day. Draw a picture that shows one way that you use energy. Describe the type of energy you are using.

31.3 Uses of Energy

90

SCIENCE

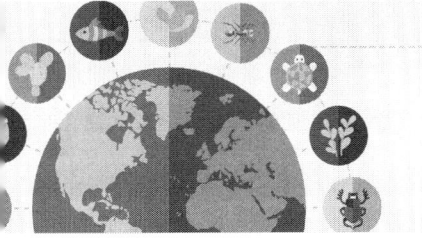

Name: _____ Date: _____

Natural vs. Man-made Resources

Directions: Use what you know about natural and man-made resources to complete the activities below.

1. Cut out the images on the next page along the dotted lines. Decide if each image shows a natural resource or a man-made resource. Paste it in the correct column in the table.

Natural Resources	Man-made Resources

2. Choose one of the man-made resources from the chart above and explain how it was created from a natural resource.

_____
_____
_____
_____

Next Page

32.1 Natural Resources

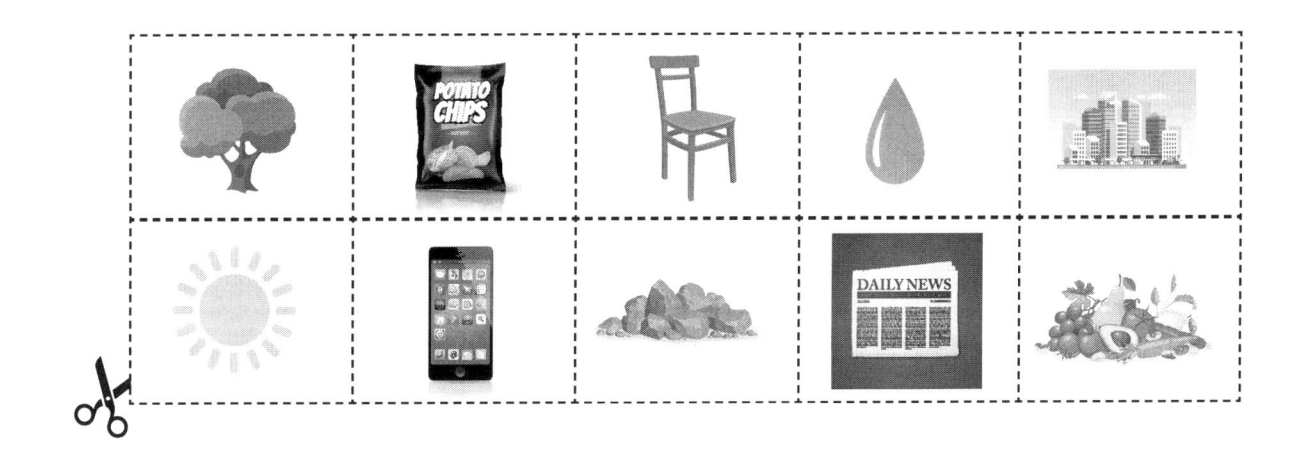

32.1 Natural Resources

SCIENCE

Name: _____ Date: _____

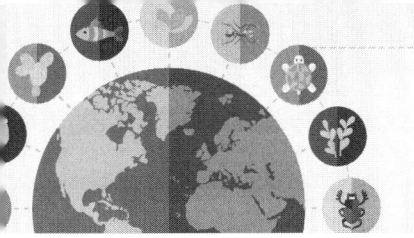

Nonrenewable Resource Uses

Directions: Cut out the images on the next page along the dotted lines. Paste each picture in the table next to the nonrenewable resource that describes it. Complete the table by listing some uses for each nonrenewable resource.

Nonrenewable Resource	Picture	Uses
rocks and minerals		
oil		
natural gas		

Next Page

32.2 Nonrenewable Resources

96

metal		
coal		

32.2 Nonrenewable Resources

SCIENCE

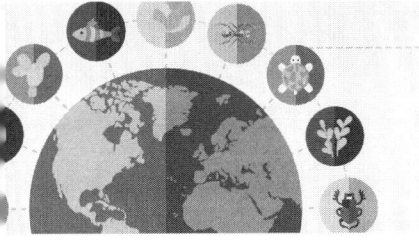

Name: _____ Date: _____

Products Made From Living Things

Directions: Show how products are made from living things. Cut out the pictures on the next page along the dotted lines. Paste the correct items in the correct order to complete each diagram.

1. Paste pictures in the boxes to show how ice cream is made from cows.

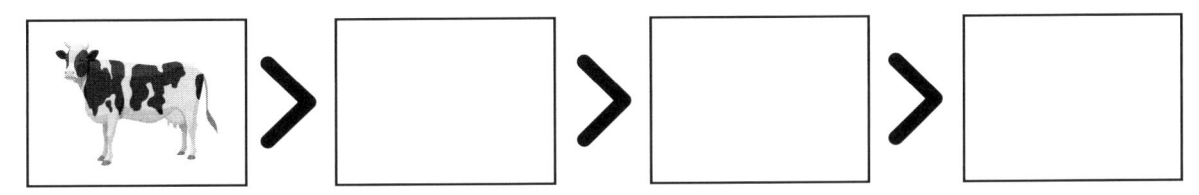

2. Paste pictures in the boxes to show how a blanket is made from sheep.

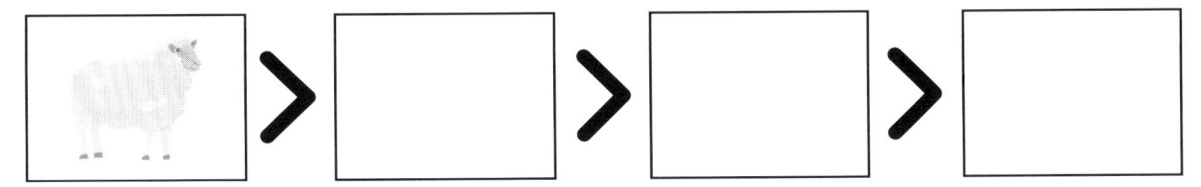

3. Paste pictures in the boxes to show how a shirt is made from cotton plants.

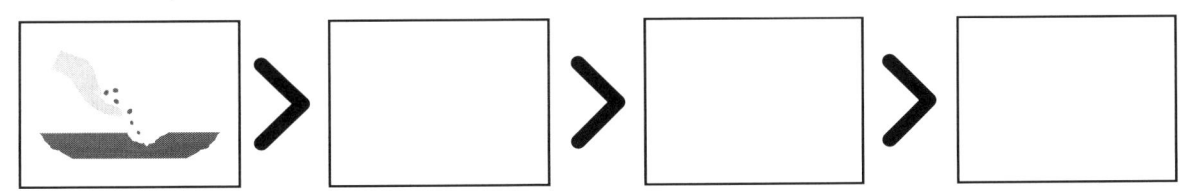

4. Paste pictures in the boxes to show how paper is made from trees.

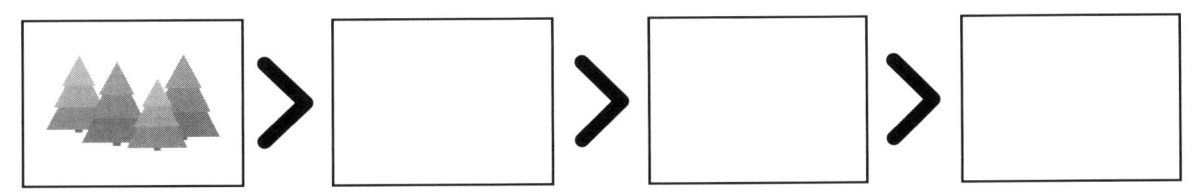

Next Page

33.1 Human Made Resources

33.1 Human Made Resources

SCIENCE

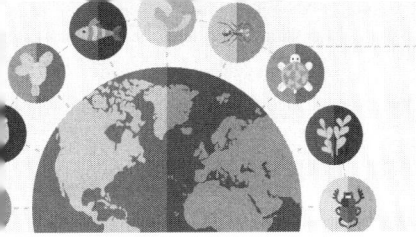

Name: _____ Date: _____

Uses of Technology

Directions: Practice identifying technologies and how they are used by matching them to the correct use. Cut out the pictures and text along the dotted lines on the next page. Paste the pictures and text in the correct places in the chart.

Technology	Picture	Use
washing machine		
television		
computer		

Next Page

33.2 Technology

104

refrigerator		
telephone		
headphones		

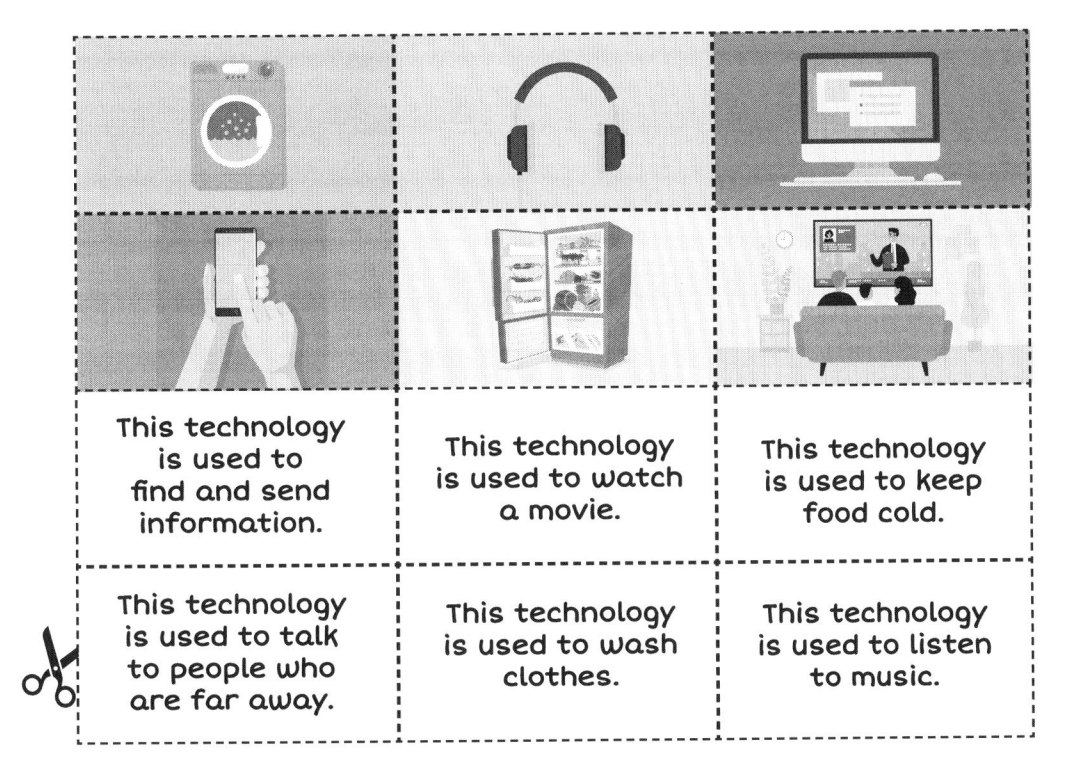

This technology is used to find and send information.

This technology is used to watch a movie.

This technology is used to keep food cold.

This technology is used to talk to people who are far away.

This technology is used to wash clothes.

This technology is used to listen to music.

33.2 Technology

SCIENCE

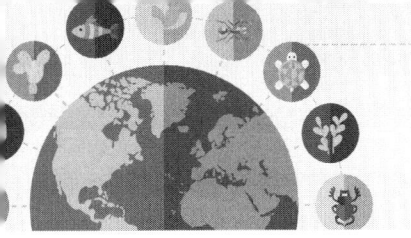

Name: _____ Date: _____

Helpful or Harmful

Directions: Cut out the pictures on the next page along the dotted lines. Decide whether each picture shows a way to be helpful or harmful to the Earth and its natural resources. Paste each picture in the correct column.

Helpful Examples	Harmful Examples

Next Page

33.3 Conserving Resources

33.3 Conserving Resources

SCIENCE

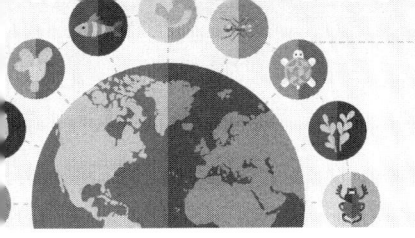

Name: _____ Date: _____

Natural Resource Product Book

Directions: For this project, you will create a flipbook that shows things that can be made from natural resources. Cut out the pictures below along the dotted lines. Next, paste each image on the correct page of your flipbook according to the natural resource that is being used. Finally, draw two more examples for each natural resource. Once completed, cut out and arrange the pages like the example on the next page and staple the flipbook at the top.

Next Page

33.4 Project: Natural Resource Product Book

Example of flipbook

Natural Resource
Product Book

- Water
- Cotton
- Animals
- Trees

Natural Resource
Product Book

Next Page

33.4 Project: Natural Resource Product Book

Water

Cotton

Next Page

33.4 Project: Natural Resource Product Book

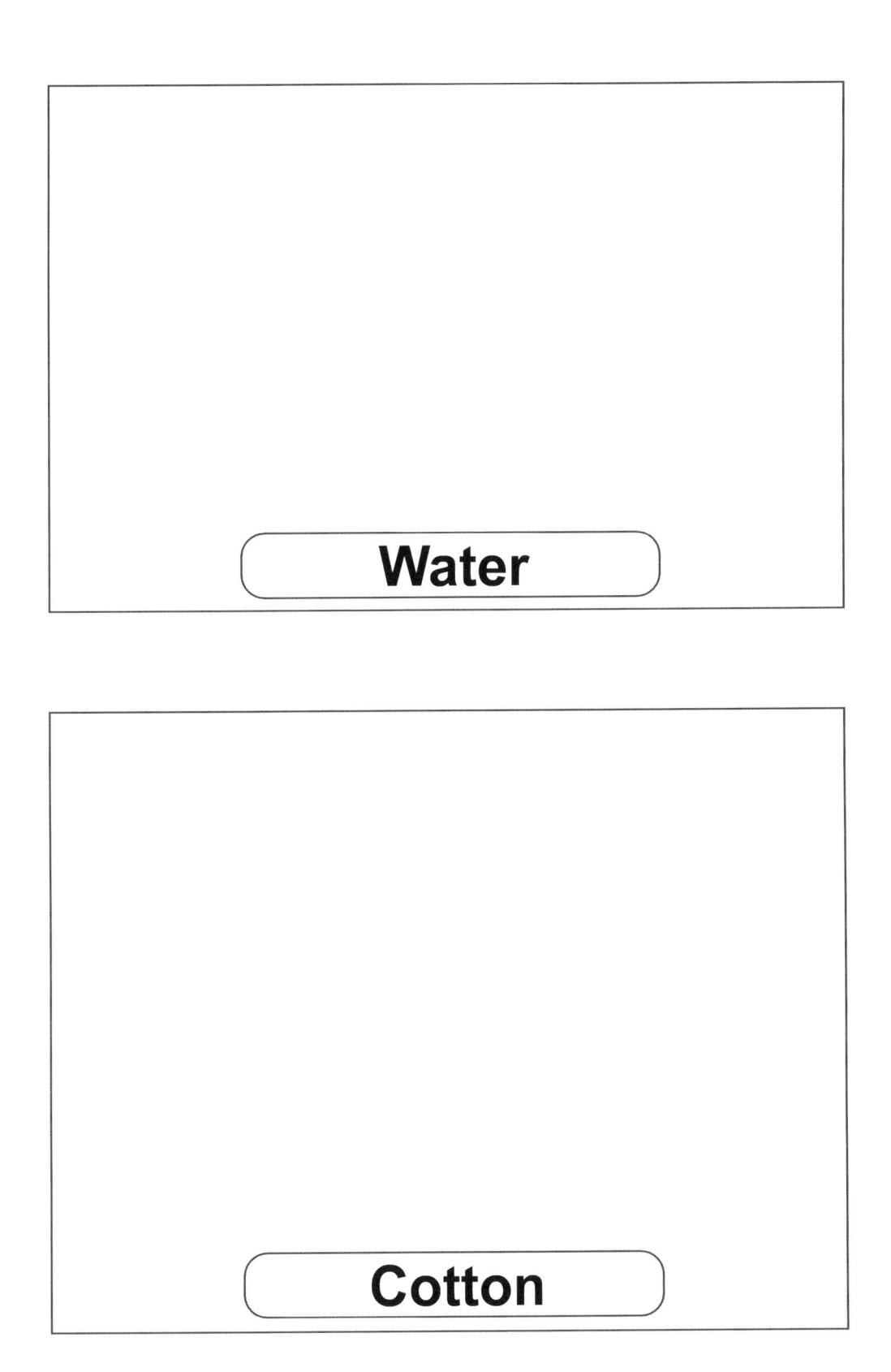

116

Animals

33.4 Project: Natural Resource Product Book

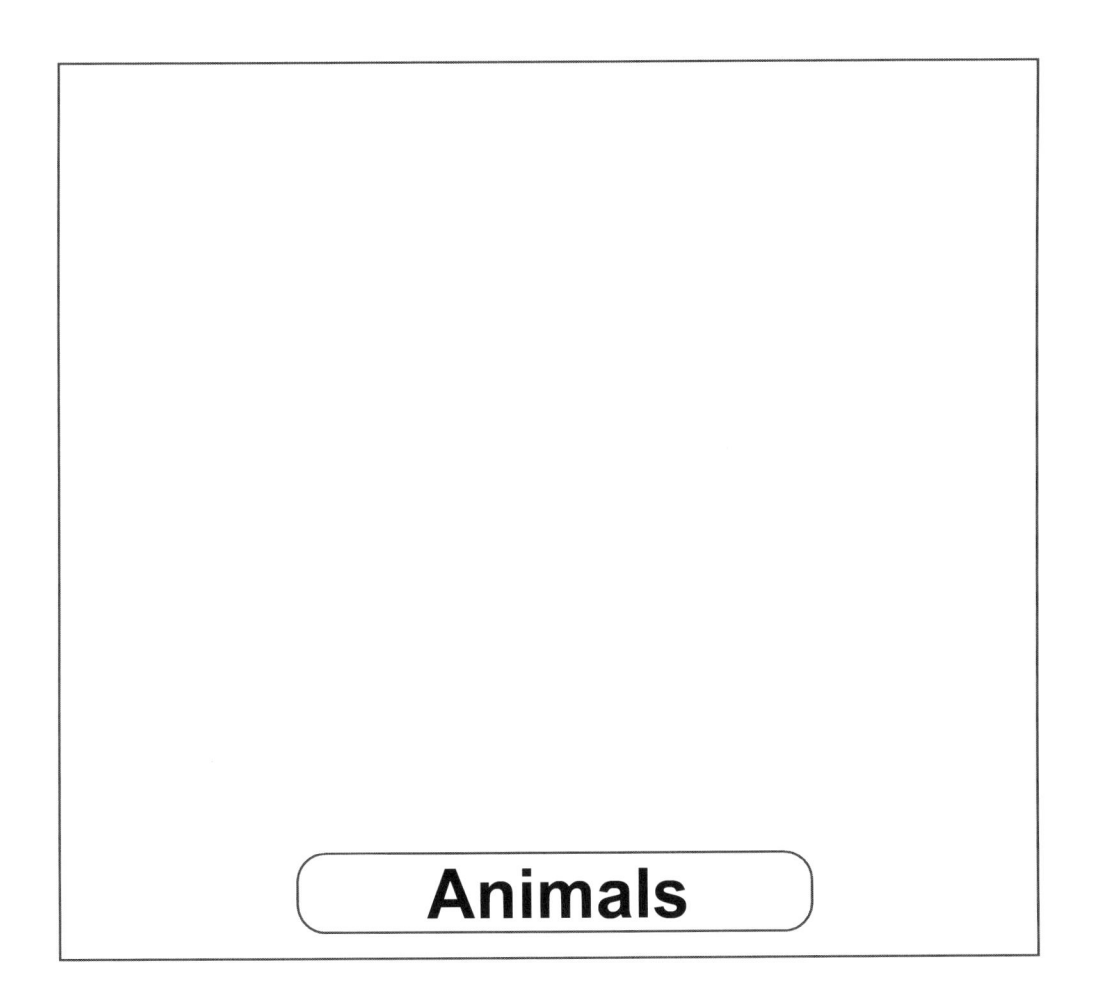

Trees

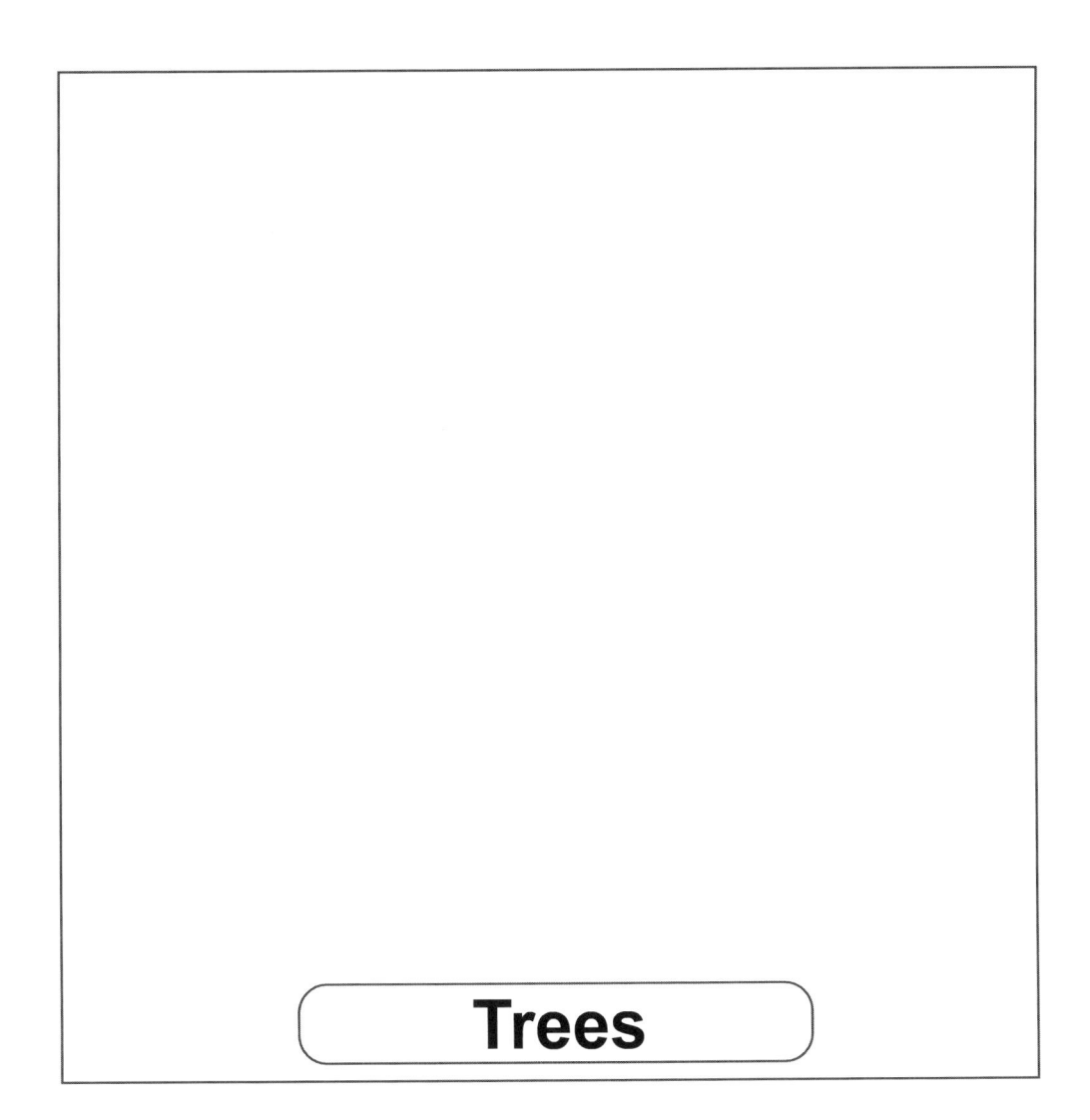

SCIENCE

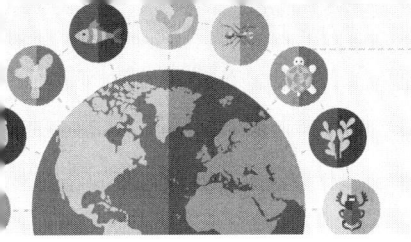

Name: _____   Date: _____

Pollution Effects

Directions: Cut out the pictures on the next page along the dotted lines. Paste each one in the correct row according to what kind of pollution it shows. Then write at least TWO effects of each type of pollution.

	Image	Effects
air pollution		
water		
land pollution		

Next Page

34.1 Pollution   122

34.1 Pollution

SCIENCE

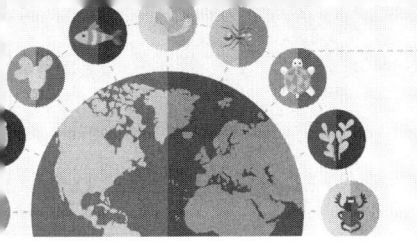

Name: _____ Date: _____

Creating Compost

Directions: Instead of throwing away food waste, use what you have learned in this lesson to plan your own compost. Answer each question below to help you plan and start creating healthy soil!

1. What kinds of foods can you put in your compost?
   _____
   _____
   _____
   _____

2. Where will you keep your compost?
   _____
   _____
   _____
   _____

3. What will be some of the results of your compost pile?
   _____
   _____
   _____
   _____

4. How long do you predict it will take for your compost to break down?
   _____
   _____
   _____
   _____

Next Page

35.2 Composting

5. Cut out the pictures below along the dotted lines. Paste them in the correct order to show the compost cycle.

☐ ☐ ☐ ☐

Optional: Build your compost! If you have the space and the materials, build your compost. Add any food waste to the compost over time.

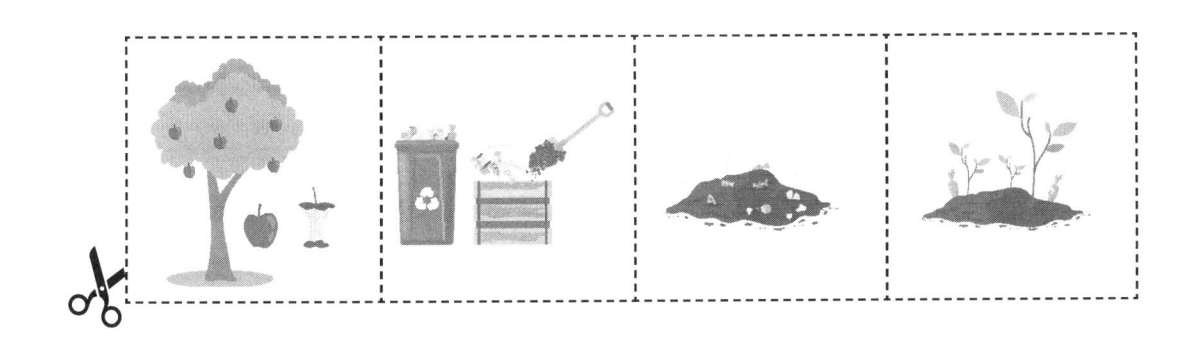

35.2 Composting

Name: _____   Date: _____

Garden Care Plan

Directions: Cut out the images along the dotted lines on the next page. Devise a plan to help care for your garden throughout the week. Each day, complete at least two tasks to help maintain your garden and keep your plants healthy. You can do the same task more than once a week. Paste the tasks that you plan to do on your weekly plan below.

Monday	Tuesday	Wednesday	Thursday	Friday	Saturday	Sunday

Next Page

35.3 Caring for Your Garden

130

remove dead plants	remove dead plants	remove dead plants	remove dead plants
check leaves	check leaves	check leaves	check leaves
watch for pests	watch for pests	watch for pests	watch for pests
pull weeds	pull weeds	pull weeds	ptull weeds
check soil	check soil	check soil	check soil
water	water	water	water

35.3 Caring for Your Garden

© 2023 by Accelerate Education
Visit us on the Web at: www.accelerate.education
ISBN: 978-1-63916-154-6